THE SHOPAHOLICS G

1970s
SHEFFIELD

By Neil Anderson

Published by
ACMЯETRO

Inside Atkinsons store on The
Moor 23rd November 1972.
Mr. Brian King, company
secretary of Atkinsons
in the foreground

ISBN: 978-0-9563649-1-3

Published by ACM Retro,
The Grange,
Church Street,
Dronfield,
Sheffield S18 1QB

Visit ACMRetro at
www.acmretro.com

Published by ACM Retro 2009

Neil Anderson asserts the moral right to be
identified as the author of this work

Acknowledgements

Sheffield Newspapers for use of their wonderful pics and articles (and particular
thanks to Jane Salt for digging them all out the archives and the girls in The Star
Shop for their mad anecdotes: Debbie Ogden, Lynda Butterell, Jackie Capper
and Joanne Stephenson), Local Studies Library for use of the pics and access to
archives, Sheffield City Council, Peter Wigley, Marie-Luise Coulthard, Rod Scott,
Gill Nour, Jan Wilson, Peter Mara, Richard Sheldon, Patricia Eales, Julie Wilson,
Tony Beesley, Chris Calow, Olga Marshall, Julie Spafford, Val Wilkinson, Sheryl
Littlewood, Angela McBroom and particular thanks to Janet Marcon.

Book design and layout: Ann Beedham

Research assistant: Emma Greendale

Sub editing: Ian Cheetham, Karen Davies and Maggie Soutar

THE SHOPAHOLICS GUIDE TO
1970s SHEFFIELD

Dedicated to Mum and Dad
who first introduced me to Redgates

LEWIS'S Jewellers

Sheffield's Chapel Walk,
28th November, 1974

Readers of The Star were asked if men were the best shoppers on November 6th 1972

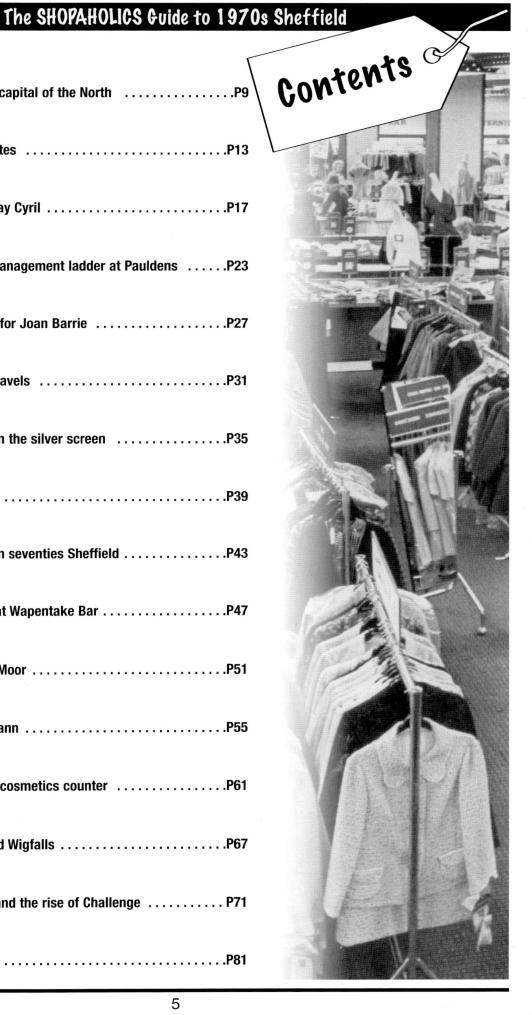

Contents

Intro:
Sheffield – shopping capital of the North P9

Chapter 1:
The wonder of Redgates .P13

Chapter 2:
Schofields and Subway Cyril P17

Chapter 3:
Bottom rung of the management ladder at Pauldens P23

Chapter 4:
Davys and modelling for Joan Barrie P27

Chapter 5:
The 'saved' shelf at Ravels P31

Chapter 6:
Steel City shopping on the silver screen P35

Chapter 7:
Sheffield 1 – Leeds 0 . . . . .P39

Chapter 8:
Where to buy music in seventies Sheffield P43

Chapter 9:
Meat and potato pie at Wapentake Bar P47

Chapter 10:
Sexy Rexy and more Moor P51

Chapter 11:
No talking at Philip Cann P55

Chapter 12:
Sweet sixteen on the cosmetics counter P61

Chapter 13:
Winning the pools and Wigfalls .P67

Chapter 14:
Christmas shopping and the rise of Challenge P71

Chapter 15:
Sheffield markets P81

Charter Square with Pauldens department store in the background

Eurovision Song Contest winner Dana signs autographs for the crowds amassed outside Pauldens

SHEFFIELD
Shopping capital of the North

Cole
Brothers
on show
at night

SHEFFIELD

Shopping Centre of the North
City of Sheffield

The mere thought of Meadowhall in the seventies would have been laughed off the high street.
It wouldn't have stood a chance. Sheffield city centre offered a shopping experience like nowhere else in the land.

People would travel from right around the region – often right across the country – to sample it.

It offered every conceivable type of shop – from resplendent department stores like Pauldens, Cockaynes and Redgates toy

shop to Christmas illuminations to rival Blackpool.

Sheffield rightly crowned itself as 'the shopping centre of the north'.

In the pre-carbon footprint world of 1972 W. E. Franklin, the then president of Sheffield and District Chamber of Trade, was boasting of the area's 10,000 car parking spaces and "more city centre multi-storey car parks in the pipeline".

There were even annual competitions to find the Lady Sales Assistant of the Year

People would travel from right around the region

15th April 1975. Beat the budget drinkers were out in force as this crowd formed at Augustus Barnett Wines and Spirits on Ecclesall Road South

Confidence in Sheffield at that point was incredible

and the Saleswomen of the Year organised by the city's Junior Chamber of Commerce in those pre-politically correct times.

Much of the success of getting the massive department stores to invest in the city was down to Sheffield City Council (or Sheffield Corporation as they were then known) and it was all part of their far-reaching plans for a new-look Steel City.

The confidence in Sheffield at that point was incredible – it was truly lining up to sell itself to the world and shed the "world-wide image of Sheffield as a row of back-to-back terraced houses punctuated by the smokiest steel works in Europe".

The size and audacity of the marketing drive seems hard to believe, even by today's standards.

In 1971 a City On The Move exhibition

was unveiled at London's Royal Exchange.

Opened by the then Lord Mayor of London, Sir Peter Studd, it was designed to bring the capital's public up to date with Sheffield.

Months in the planning, Sheffield - City On The Move ran from March 8 to 13 with the over riding aim of shattering prejudices levelled at the city.

The idea for the exhibition, thought to have been the largest of its type ever held in London's financial world up to that time, was originally conceived in September 1970 as part of a £50,000 publicity budget granted by the town hall a year earlier.

The massive undertaking touched on every aspect of Sheffield life, a thread followed by the film that followed a year later.

roberts
THE DEPARTMENT STORE

SPECIAL
OFFERS | Branded Upholstery
& FURNITURE

SHEFFIELD

City worth
seeing
City of Sheffield

But the Sheffield roadshow didn't stop in London, far from it.

A council-sponsored 500 metre stand went to Gothenburg in Sweden for the International Swedish Trade Fair from May 5-14, 1972.

Steel making and engineering giants of the city were a large part of the 70 Sheffield companies and included: Brown Bayleys, Firth Vickers, Arthur Lee, Neepsend, Laycock Engineering, Swift Levick and more.

The city had the third largest stand at the massive fair.

And far from living in the shadow of near-by cities like Leeds, Manchester and Nottingham, Sheffield took the shopping fight to them.

They blitzed Leeds with Santa-style carrier bags in a bid to bag Christmas trade

with the message – "Shop in Sheffield this Christmas!".

At one point they were in a media war with Nottingham as they argued Steel City was the true home of the master archer Robin Hood.

Over 350,000 stickers were produced in a bid to bring tourists, conference organisers, shoppers and industrialists into the city to see what it had to offer.

The first batch of ten different designs used headings such as "Emerging City", "City Of Skills And Quality" and "The Clean Air City".

It was one of the most audacious and successful PR campaigns of any city in the UK and helped totally transform the image of Sheffield and its shopping experience.

Above:
Roberts
Brothers on
The Moor.

Left:
One of the
promotional
stickers

People
would
travel from
right around
the region

The stickers designed by the Town Hall to sell seventies Sheffield to the world

Garden city of the North
City of Sheffield

Great place to live
City of Sheffield

City of skills and quality
City of Sheffield

Emerging city
City of Sheffield

Crossroads of Great Britain
City of Sheffield

For your next conference
City of Sheffield

Easy to get to city
City of Sheffield

The clean air city
City of Sheffield

Atkinsons on The Moor

The wonder of Redgates

Chapter 1

Mandy Nunn and electronic toys, Redgates 5th November 1979

Jan Wilson: Treats from Redgates

Jan Wilson, former Sheffield City Council leader, remembers Redgates in its former home in Fitzalan Square:

"Redgates in Fitzalan Square - I remember going to the dentist and Mum taking me to Redgates for a treat afterwards - presumably if I had been a brave girl.

"I was allowed to choose a small toy: the thing I remember best was the toy post office, with all the different forms and stamps.

"Suggs on Leopold Street was like a little cluttered Aladdin's cave of sports equipment. I can only remember going in to buy tennis balls and the massive glamour associated with the ones which had been used at Wimbledon and which sports shops then sold off cheap."

"Suggs on Leopold Street was like a little Aladdin's cave."
Jan Wilson

Redgates BIG BIG TOY STORE

PRAMS

FATHER CHRISTMAS GROTTO

CHILDREN'S CLOTHES

Hot Wheels

THE FASTEST CARS IN THE WORLD

STOP PRESS !

Take advantage of the wonderful savings on Hot Wheels prices. Ask for leaflets giving full details.

Sizzlers ™

WITH A BUILT-IN MOTOR!

MATTEL

See the SIZZLERS demonstrated along with many others too numerous to list.

No Christmas is complete without a visit to our store.

Redgates

ESTABLISHED·1857

THE LARGEST SELECTION OF TOYS IN ENGLAND

18-24 · FURNIVAL GATE : MOORHEAD : SHEFFIELD S13LE : TELEPHONE 77585
OPEN 6 DAYS A WEEK
Toys and prams are also obtainable from our branch at
56 KNIFESMITHGATE : CHESTERFIELD : Telephone 4514

Neil Anderson:

Neil Anderson: "A visit to Redgates was an almost mythical experience. I remember going in at Christmas with my brother and parents. My dad disappeared for a while and reappeared with these massive Redgates bags – the ones with the red logos all over them – and we were going mental to know what was in them and he was just smiling, knowingly.

"We were just on the cusp of deciding whether Santa or the parents were behind Christmas – it was mix of intrigue but mainly just excitement!

"I remember going in week after week buying one or two soldiers at a time, spending hours gawping into those fantastic displays behind glass cases.

"One of my favourite buys – and I presume my dad ended up actually making these as always happened – was when one of the model companies branched out into horror movies and you could actually buy The Wolf Man and Dracula: I was over the moon!

"I think my grandma had just started extolling the virtues of Bela Lugosi and Lon Chaney Junior.

"I'm sure the Dracula model ended up on Salem's Lot a few years later and I started turning the house over looking for mine, obviously to no avail.

"I also remember getting the mad Pink Panther car, the one that seemed to be virtually indestructible and would travel at approx 110 miles an hour thanks to this inner cog/plastic zip you used to pull and you just launched the thing. It was mad.

"It might have been indestructible but it has still gone.

"And then there was the day Action Man developed 'gripping hands': that was another Christmas sewn up.

Bring back Redgates!

"And how much Subbuteo did we buy year after year, mostly because you only had to look at it before it broke.

"But you didn't mind because you could buy the whole new football strip, new floodlights and every other possible add-on to this brilliantly conceived money-spinning brand.

"I remember we'd already visited the hallowed ground that was Hamleys in London prior to their brief stop off in Sheffield.

"In the bat of an eyelid (well time seemed liked that when you were a kid) we'd gone from having not one but TWO of the best toyshops in the entire Western World. Shame they managed to cancel each other out and we ended up with none whatsoever.

Redgates in all its glory

"So yes, in terms of a magical childhood, Redgates was totally where it was at.

"Floor upon floor of every conceivable toy, either behind a glass case or you got an all-singing, all-dancing demo.

"Forget Toys R Us, it's a soulless aircraft hangar. If you want toys there's only one place that ever truly brought them alive – bring back Redgates!"

Operation Airlift: German visitors go shopping for toys in Walshs. 26th May, 1973

The Moor, Sheffield

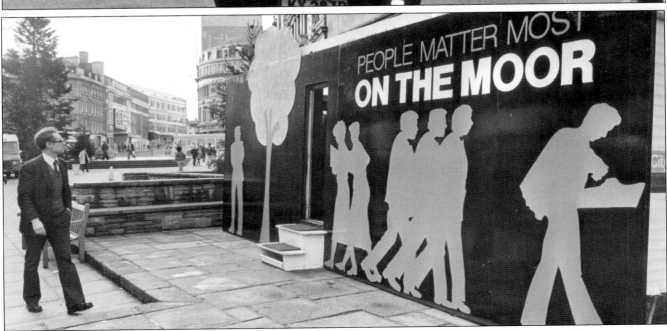

The Moor pedestrianisation scheme caravan in Fargate, Sheffield. 8th January, 1979

Schofields and Subway Cyril

Chapter 2

Peter Mara in his days as head chef at Schofields

"Saturdays were definitely the most buzzing time to be shopping in Sheffield city centre: Schofields, Debenhams, Walshs, Cole Brothers – there were no £1 shops then."

Peter Mara

Peter Mara: Head Chef at Schofields

Peter Mara: "I was head chef at Schofields department store [the shop that replaced Cockaynes] in the 1970s. It was a very busy place with a large kitchen brigade, the size of which you will only see in a five-star London hotel these days.

"We had an upstairs restaurant overlooking Angel Street. The self-service restaurant was a 200-seater and we also had a 96-seat á la carte.

"We had 14 chefs. The á la carte restaurant was a daily changing menu. The self-service restaurant boasted a fish counter, a roast counter and a 'wet' counter, which included curry and rice and so on.

"Everything was fresh.

The manager was Mrs Lomas.

"Schofields even had its own deli on Hartshead, occupied by Churchills now.

"The whole of the Hartshead area was so busy.

"I remember the busiest Saturday we ever had in the restaurant - we ended up having to send across to Walshs for more potatoes: we used eight sacks that day on chips alone!

"It seems hard to believe now that you could be that busy in a department store.

"There were 36 of us in total in the catering department.

"I met my first wife nearby: she ran the Danish Kitchen which was above Hornes where

I had my shirts made.

"There was nowhere quite like the Danish Kitchen at that point, there were no pies and puddings there. It was quite revolutionary for its time, with lots of Danish pastries, cold meats, salad and filter coffee.

"Back at Schofields we'd regularly serve oysters, duck, beef, game pie and rib of beef.

"Departments included perfumery, clothing, kitchenware, handbags, bed linen and more.

"As a member of staff you got 12.5% discount: I got my wife some Carmen Rollers as a gift.

"To give you an example of size, we also had a separate kitchen that just did meals for staff, which would be doing 100 to 200 lunches.

"I remember buying my first colour television from Bunker and Pratley who were based in the Hole in the Road.

"I still can't remember a day when all the escalators worked – even in the early days – but I can vividly recall the man nicknamed Subway Cyril.

"He was a tramp but he was what I'd call an 'old school' tramp. He didn't bother anyone. I think a chip shop on The Wicker fed him.

"Saturdays were definitely the most buzzing time to be shopping in Sheffield city centre: Schofields, Debenhams, Walshs, Cole Brothers – there were no £1 shops then."

Peter Mara today

Spend Christmas with Peter Dominic.

Apart from these Christmas bargains (and a lot more besides), you'll get super service all round.

Every one of our branches has a manager who knows his stuff backwards and is always happy to give advice and answer your queries.

He can tell you anything, from what will go best with the turkey, pud, or whatever, to the sort of tipple Uncle Charlie would appreciate as a gift.

So if you're looking for value, visit one of our friendly wineshops today.

PETER DOMINIC
ALL THE WORLD'S WINES

Well, would you let your husband wear tights?

THE STAR ...WITH AN EYE FOR THE UNUSUAL!

GADZOOKS SIR — 'twas a cold day for a frolick in Fargate.

And, said madame, it was something to be seen to be believed.

But all was not what it seemed. . . .

It was the day 1972-MAN, in the shape of reporter John Honeywell, made his debut in the latest "gear" — coloured tights for men.

He could have worn them under his trousers of course, as the retailers recommend — for keeping warm while skiing or taking part in other outdoor pursuits.

But the only pursuits in Fargate occurred when a group of housewives visiting the city from Leeds took a fancy to him.

If you don't fancy the shocking pink pair worn by John, they are also available in green and blue — though at £1.50 they're a bit pricier than women's tights.

What does Honeywell have to say about his adventure?

"Ballet dancing has never appealed to me — partly because male ballet dancers look so ridiculous in tights.

But yesterday I was thrust into Fargate looking for all the world like an overweight Nureyev — except for the size 10 boots on my feet.

For just £1.50 the male with the peacock instinct can look like John Honeywell

Outlook grim

Oh, quite ducky!

The biggest drawback was pulling them up to fit properly.

And, out in the street, I grew accustomed to the

Whatever next!

sly glances, hoots of laughter and wolf-whistles. It was the icy cold wind that drove me back inside again.

A GROUP of housewives out shopping just had to find out more about the latest in gents' mod gear.

"AWFUL," said Mrs. Carol Taylor, aged 22, of Edenhall Road, Arbourthorne, Sheffield, in between fits of laughter, adding: "I wouldn't let my husband be seen dead them."

"They look like dyed long johns to me — what a mess. I wouldn't even consider wearing them myself," said 67-year-old Mr. Harold Skellern, of Victoria Road, Bamford.

"YES, I would let my husband wear them but I think I would prefer yellow to shocking pink," said Mrs. Susan Coupe, aged 25, of Bramley Lane, Handsworth, Sheffield.

"I'M staggered," confessed Mrs. Margaret Sargent, aged 29, of Ecclesall Road South, Sheffield, adding as an afterthought, "I should think they are quite warm though."

An article from The Sheffield Star newspaper of Wednesday, December 8th, 1971

Seventies
advertising post

Bottom rung of the management ladder at Pauldens

Chapter 3

Women and children's fashion floor at Pauldens

Richard Sheldon: Memories of Pauldens

"I was just 17 years old. My title was trainee department manager on a wage of £6.40 a week for a 42 hour week."

Richard Sheldon

Outside cafe area at Pauldens

"I started work at Pauldens in September 1970 having left Dinnington High School in that summer - it was my first job after leaving school.

"I was just 17 years old. My title was trainee department manager on a wage of £6.40 a week for a 42 hour week.

"The hours were 9am until 5.30pm, Friday late night until 7.30pm and Saturday until 6pm.

"We went metric not long after and one of the first jobs I did was to dual price merchandise showing decimal price and old money to help customers convert. What a task, they were all hand-written signs!

"I started out on the footwear department selling shoes in the old way - sitting customers down, bringing box after box out of the stockroom for trying on and hoping to find something they liked.

"I remember serving the Bishop of Sheffield who wanted to buy some slippers, he had half the stockroom out and kept calling me "my dear boy". He was obviously used to being served hand and foot if you pardon the pun!

"I soon discovered why all the lady assistants had their till keys on a piece of elastic fastened to their waist.

"You had to put the key in the till to open it and if you forgot to take it out and walked away the elastic stretched and no damage was done.

"I put mine on a piece of string (clever sod), forgot to take my key out and walked away leaving most of my ripped trouser leg hanging from the till!

"I ended up getting one of the girls in the alter- ations room to stick me back together. I couldn't have looked too bad though as we ended up dating. It must have been my bare leg that swung it!

"The store was typical of the old-fashioned way of staffing with floor walkers or managers, responsible for a whole floor of the store, assistant floor managers, department managers, assistant department managers, salesmen, then the lowest of all, the trainee managers (us!)

"We didn't get commission on what we sold, but the salesmen did, so they were quite matey with you hoping you would key in their staff number when you sold something so they got the commission.

"I remember the store manager was Mr Lofthouse who always raised his hat to you on the staff stairs

if he saw you in a morning - I always felt honoured.

"The staff canteen was always a scrum to get served as we only had a 10 minute break in the morning and it was quite a walk to get there.

"I do remember one day looking out of the window and all of a sudden a huge crane collapsed on a construction site opposite, smashing to the floor.

"Quite a few of the staff were upset about it.

"We had to clock on before 9am to get to our station to be ready for store opening.

"I lived at Todwick Village, about 11 miles away from Sheffield with only one bus per hour to Pond Street Bus Station in the city centre.

"Problem was I had to get down The Moor for 9am and the 8 o'clock bus only got me into town for 9am so I ended up having to get the 7am.

"That got me into town for 8am and I ended up having to sit in the Peace Gardens for an hour waiting to clock on to ensure I wouldn't be late - now there's old fashioned commitment eh!

"The late finish on a Friday (7.30pm) meant a dash for the No. 15 bus from Pond Street. It left at 8 o'clock and got me home for 9pm.

"It was a very long day and I used to see my mates getting off the bus to go out to town as I was getting on it to go home.

"They thought I was mad working in a shop with daft hours, they all worked down the pit or in steel/engineering - but all their places of work ended up shutting down in years to come and I'm still going, more luck than judgement I suppose.

"I remember a few characters from the store. One was the toilet attendant/cleaner called Tom who had previously worked for a removals firm in Sheffield. He would have us in stiches with tales of loose women and all sorts of goings on during his days as a removal man. Facinating stuff when you're only 17 and just starting out in life.

"In many ways your first job helps shape your working life as you aspire to be like some of your fellow work mates. You looked up to and respected most (not all) of them.

"Life was never dull down on The Moor. We had lunch sometimes at Wapentake Bar or The Nelson close by."

Above: Richard Sheldon in the early seventies

Below: Richard Sheldon as he is now

Davy's and modelling for Joan Barrie

Fargate in 1979

Fargate in 1973

Patricia Glover (now Eales):

"There was no better smell in the world than that of the fresh coffee being ground by Davy's Cafe on Fargate – I used to look forward to it every time I went near the place.

"As a special treat I'd go to their restaurant upstairs. It was very nice and you always had waitress service – there was no self-service. I remember there was really nice décor, it was all dark wood panelling.

"I used to have a Saturday job working in Joan Barrie and I also modelled for them when they had fashion shows in the shop.

"Going shopping in Sheffield city centre was a real outing.

"I always remember gazing through the thick glass of the very expensive furriers called Marshall & Snellgrove that had amazing bow-shaped windows.

"People used to get so dressed up to go shopping in the city centre in the seventies. The elderly ladies were always so resplendent in their hats.

"I was too young to be wearing a hat, especially if I'd had my hair done at

Relaxing in in the sun on Fargate, 1976

Laid away at Cockaynes

George France on Chapel Walk or Herchelle above Castle Square roundabout.

"Saturday afternoon was my time for a weekly visit to Sheffield city centre. I couldn't go in the week because I was working at Firth Vickers in the East End.

"My first stop of any visit would be Peter Robinson's, they always had some fantastic items in there.

"But my favourite two shops were always Walshs or Cockaynes department stores. They were great family shops and I used to love the

make-up section in Cockaynes.

"That shop was so high-class and posh, definitely up a notch from Cole Brothers.

Patricia Glover in the seventies

"I remember my Auntie Harriet used to go every single week and she'd always have something 'laid away' and come

Patricia today

back to pay for it the week after. You just can't imagine doing that anymore.

"But one thing I never had much time for was the Hole In the Road. I thought it was an absolute waste of time and it caused more traffic issues than it solved."

Tramps of
King Street

The 'saved' shelf at Ravels

Chapter 5

"There was a real social scene to shopping in the city centre."
Julie Wilson

Hole in The Road with its famous fish tank (right)

Cockaynes department store

Young Rascals

Julie Wilson:

"I started work as a Saturday girl in Ravel Shoes near the top of Fargate in the late seventies around the time I was doing A-levels.

I had a fantastic time but the manageress – 'poison dwarf' she was referred to as – always had me doing all the horrible jobs.

"I'd have to spend hours in the massive stockroom putting all the boxes of shoes in order before she checked them all personally.

"Ravels was such a cool shop at that time. I remember Human League's Phil Oakey and ABC's Martin Fry both used to be regular customers.

"In the long run working there was no good for me at all: it gave me a taste for very expensive shoes and handbags!

"It was definitely the Russell & Bromley of its day.

"There was a real social scene to shopping in the city centre at that period. Customers would come and cruise around the shop; it was like they were in a fashion parade.

"Another of my first bosses, Ingrid, had the

"There was a real social scene at Ravel and nearby shops like Western Jean Company."

Above:
Julie Wilson
in Ravels

Left:
Western Jean
Company in Fargate

Saturday girl at Ravel Shoes

most amazing lop-sided wedge hairstyle, long before Phil Oakey had it. If her hair wasn't totally straight she wouldn't allow us to open the shop until it was.

"Though there was no set uniform we were all expected to dress well. Ravel Shoes was definitely an 'in' place to work at that point.

"I remember my friend Jayne getting a job at a nearby shoe shop and being very upset that she wasn't at Ravel.

"I eventually became shop manager at Ravel. At one point the favourite

"Another of my first bosses, Ingrid, had the most amazing lop-sided wedge hairstyle, long before Phil Oakey had it".

style of the entire shop was a pair of black, patent leather, high-heeled court shoes at £29.99 – a lot of money in the late 1970s.

"But we were also a bit naughty and would put our favourite shoes on the 'saved' shelf and wait

for them to be reduced in the sale.

"We also had 25% staff discount. I remember ending up with a pair of boots that started out at £75 and I got them for next to nothing in the end!

"There was a real social scene at Ravel and nearby shops like Western Jean Company. We'd regularly get ready in the staff room and go straight out after the shop shut at night to bars like the Blue Bell on High Street that used to open quite early.

"It wasn't unusual for

our shop workers to end up sleeping in the staff room if they were a bit worse for wear and had to get up early to be back at work!

"I remember we used to regularly have bacon sandwiches ordered from Lynne's Pantry on Surrey Street and we'd go to Wimpy on Fargate for lunch.

"Christmas was always a great time. We'd have bottles of Babycham sent up and down in the goods' lift for staff: the manager at the time knew nothing about that..."

Steel City shopping on the silver screen

Chapter 6

Filming The Reel
Monty/City On
The Move

Reel Monty: Peter Wigley's City On The Move

He devised and implemented probably the most audacious and successful PR campaigns of any northern city in the history of tourism and commerce

The job of selling Sheffield's shopping experience to the world lay at the feet of one man, Peter Wigley.

He was the city's first-ever publicity officer and started at the Town Hall in 1969.

He devised and implemented probably the most audacious and successful PR campaign of any northern city in the history of tourism and commerce.

The crowning glory of the promotional drive was his City On The Move flick, the film that fronts The Full Monty and brings to life the swinging city of the early 1970s, boasting long-gone civic icons like the Hole in the Road - an award-winning subterranean, pedestrian area complete with shops, tropical fish tank and all-weather escalators; The Fiesta - the biggest nightclub in Europe that once held a date open for Elvis (he never arrived); the "streets in the sky" of the then ground-breaking Park Hill Flats complex; Sheffield Show in its hey-day and the Millhouses Park lido.

Peter Wigley, who is now 77 years old and still lives in the city, said at the time of the promotional film's launch:

"They might learn that Sheffield is not in the middle of a barren waste of the industrial night-mare but on the doorstep of the Peak District National Park; they might learn that it has the cleanest atmosphere of any industrial city in Europe.

"They might be surprised at the extent and variety of the city's parks; at the housing developments and progress in slum clearance."

The City On The Move film – now re-titled The Reel Monty and released on DVD last year - presents this great British city with the world in its sights, totally oblivious to the cruel twist of fate that was to decimate its then booming steel industry and throw tens of

Peter Wigley today, with the famous film which is now available on DVD, nearly forty years after he originally commisiioned it

thousands on the dole within a few years.

In fact Wigley's pioneering work – which brings to life the city centre shopping experience of the early 1970s - would have been consigned to the archives if it hadn't been for one of the most incredible stories in British movie history.

In 1997, after a long search, the makers of the promo flick were tracked down by a film company planning a low-budget movie about a bunch of redundant steel workers turning to stripping for a living.

Jim and Marie-Luise Coulthard, who had produced and directed the project for Mr Wigley, pleased with the interest in their film after all this time, gladly accepted the company's offer of £400 for the rights to use some of their footage.

By the time The Full Monty received its fifth Oscar nomination, the couple had helped 20th Century Fox gross over £180m.

Many moviegoers assumed that The Reel Monty footage that fronts The Full Monty was a spoof but they were very wrong.

Brendan Moffet, director of strategic marketing at Creative Sheffield and the man now tasked with managing the city's image, said:

"This was such a significant film when it was released and it's amazing how many of the messages still ring true today - especially about lifestyle and liveability within the city.

"But it's also true to say that the Sheffield of today also faces many very different challenges within the global market place as it competes for investment."

More information from www.thereelmonty.com

Below: Filming The Reel Monty/City On The Move. Picture includes Peter Wigley (second from right), director Jim Coulthard (far right), film editor Marie-Luise Coulthard (third from right) and Barry Fenn (third from left).

Sheffield 1 - Leeds 0

Chapter 7

Pinstone Street
in December
1972

CHEEKY SHEFFIELD TO WOO LEEDS SHOPPERS

By a staff reporter

THE OLD Yorkshire rivalry between Sheffield and Leeds looks like taking on a new lease of life next week. In one of their cheekiest stunts yet, Sheffield's Publicity Department are planning to give away the city's special Christmas shopping bags in the centre of Leeds.

Two promotion girls will go to Leeds, probably on Tuesday, to hand out the bags which urge people to shop in Sheffield and see the Christmas lights.

The promotion will also take in Wakefield and Huddersfield, and will mean the distribution of some 2,000 shopping bags.

Rivalry

The scheme was given the go-ahead yesterday by Sheffield's publicity Advisory Committee, and is bound to cause greater rivalry between the two cities.

Ald. Reg. Munn, chairman of the committee, said: "The shopping bags will be mainly distributed in Leeds, and are aimed at drawing attention to Sheffield shopping facilities and illuminations."

Left: Article about the Sheffield / Leeds rivalry

Right: The latest TVs in the seventies

Jackie Capper: Gladrags

"I used to go to Gladrags in the market but there was no changing room and you had to hide behind the clothing racks when you were getting undressed!

"They had all the latest gear like you'd get in London, they had all the glam stuff.

"I also used to like Harringtons. I'd go there to get my crombie, Fred Perry skirt and jacket.

"When I got older I started shopping at Chelsea Girl."

"I used to go to the Top Rank on a Saturday afternoon.

"If you were young you went in the morning, I think it was the 13 to 17 year olds in the afternoon."

Peter Wigley: Getting one over on Leeds

Peter Wigley, Sheffield's first publicity officer, who started at the Town Hall in 1969, said:

"Sheffield and Leeds had always been enemies in terms of who had the best of everything and things came to a head in the early 1970s when the BBC TV did a programme to find out which city was best.

"We were always trying to get one over on each other and in this particular year I had some carrier bags made which said 'Shop In Sheffield This Christmas'.

"Our plan was to sell them to local retailers in the city centre. We had 10,000 printed but only ended up selling 9,000 so we had 1,000 left.

"Then we had a brainwave and decided to take them up to Leeds and distribute them there.

"We got a couple of girls from the office in miniskirts and packed them off to West Yorkshire and they were literally swamped with people wanting the carrier bags.

"The same day we were contacted by Bob Langley from the Nationwide programme who asked if they could come up and film Sheffield's illuminations. I said no problem and also told them what we were doing in Leeds and they decided to extend the programme to fit that in as well.

"Our friends in Leeds were not best pleased as you can imagine! It's fair to say Sheffield won that Christmas!

"We were also responsible for launching a lot of events to retain interest in the city centre.

"Our annual 'Dancing In The Streets' was a fantastic event. I remember we somehow persuaded Dana to perform with her full band one dinnertime behind Pauldens only a few days after she won the Eurovision Song Contest.

"There was a real buzz around shopping in Sheffield city centre at that time.

"I wasn't a big shopper myself but I did get a lot of my clothes from Hornes."

"Sheffield and Leeds had always been enemies in terms of who had the best of everything and things came to a head in the early 1970s when the BBC TV did a programme to find out which city was best."

Below: Peter Wigley's Sheffield is ready to take on the world in the early 1970s

CENTRE & SUBURBS

E TRUE STORY

ERY DIRECTION

CHANGING CITY SHEFFIELD PA

"The same day we were contacted by Bob Langley from the Nationwide programme who asked if they could come up and film Sheffield's illuminations."

Peter Wigley

Where to buy music in seventies Sheffield

Chapter 8

Violet May record shop, Matilda Street, May 1978

Tony Beesley: Punk and shopping at Virgin

Above:
Tony Beesley now

Below:
Tony Beesley then

"I recall their hardly disguised disdain to us little donkey-jacketed, Doc Marten-wearing, busby-sweatered punk kids with haircuts like Dickensian urchins."

Tony Beesley

Tony Beesley: "Me and my mates discovered the joys of the seventies' Sheffield shopping experience right in the middle of the punk era. Throughout the dark days of late 1976 and through the sunny days of summer 1977 our musical tastes had not quite reached the full-on blitz of punk rock but we were well on our way by the end of that so-called summer of hate.

"Our record-buying and all things retail until that point was restricted almost entirely to the good old town of Rotherham, back in the days when music shops, toy stores and many shops of great interest to young kids were still aplenty to choose from. Soon, though, it would be the lure of the No 69 bus and many memorable journeys to the delights of the Steel City that would be a regular occurrence for us young aspiring punk and new wave kids. It seemed like every weekend and a great chunk of most school holidays was spent trawling through the uncountable array of Sheffield record shops between 1978 and 1979. And what bargains and exciting picture-covered, garishly coloured vinyl bags of plastic we brought home with us on those record-hunting day-trips.

"I think the first batch of punk 45s I bought from Sheffield were from the Virgin shop right at the bottom of The Moor. The records would have been Elvis Costello and the Attractions, Blondie, Squeeze, Lurkers and Generation X. The sales assistants in there were obnoxious 70s hippy throwbacks, the kind that knew everything about music and you could never question their musical integrity. Yeah man! Were we impressed by their encyclopaedic record-breaking superiority of knowing everything that could be needed to know in music? Were we 'eck as like!

"I recall their hardly disguised disdain to us little donkey-jacketed, Doc Marten-wearing, busby-sweatered punk kids with haircuts like Dickensian urchins... lo and behold, you can imagine their response to our plea for those car-park sized promo posters that they were about to throw out. Nevertheless, we still bought plenty of records from that local branch of Branson's empire, though not half as many as we would buy from the cheapie shops, those shops that sold singles for 25p and sometimes less, not-long-since released punk LP flops like The Jolt, Rich Kids, Cyanide and others for a quid and bags of singles for 75p where you didn't know what you were getting without some very careful and crafty improvisation while the shop staff were distracted by one of the lads nicking badges. We were never that flushed with cash so hunting for cheapos was a habit of our generation.

"I can't remember all of the names of the record shops in Sheffield but I can still recall where they all were.

"Straight off the No 69 from Rotherham, which back then stopped off at the bridge near where Ponds Forge sports centre is now, we would go down to Revolution records at the top of the Gallery near Castle Market. As you walked in there, the place was really dark.

The Moor roundabout, 1971

"It was so small you had to wait what seemed like ages to look through the bargain box on the floor near the counter.

"At the side of the door as you walked in there was a hand-written list of all the punk, new wave and interesting singles that had been released since punk's inception. Some were crossed through in biro.

"These were ones that had been deleted and were no longer available to buy. The guys who worked in the shop were a few years older than us and were what we would respectfully term proper punks. They looked like they could have been in The Clash and a few years later I saw these fellas play in a band of their own supporting some famous punk band at the Lyceum. They were a lot cooler than the hairy bunch down at the bottom of The Moor. Some memorable bargains we picked up from there were the first two Boys' LPs, The Saints' Eternally Yours LP,

Damned's Music for Pleasure and my mate Pete's discovery, the Suburban Studs LP, now highly collectable but back then a quid out of his paper-round money... Pete sold it for 20p a few years later.

"Our next vinyl stop-offs would be the old Woolworth's just around the corner, where we would very rarely actually buy anything but occasionally might buy a new wave single that had

reached the bottom end of the charts and was now in the cheapo section.

"Onwards after that would most likely be the Hole in the Road, which had a great record shop: I think it may have been k & d records.

"One Saturday afternoon in mid 1979 a bunch of us almost cleared out their punk and new wave stock that was ridiculously priced so cheap we couldn't dare refuse to buy, no matter what colour vinyl the record or how collectable or not it would become in later years or whether even we had heard of the actual band performing; it went swiftly into our bags and boosted our rapidly growing collections. What could be better than that?

"The other shops would be the handful on Chapel Walk. One was part of a department store which

had a sizeable downstairs record dept. You could ask to hear the LP you had in your hands before buying and I remember doing just that with the first Generation X LP. They also sold imported versions.

"So my versions of the first Skids and Stiff Little Fingers LPs are minus the inner sleeves and were built in España. The others on Chapel Walk were typical pop-orientated chart shops with boxes of badges and patches, stickers and clear-out priced singles on the counter.

"Another shop was situated on Fargate across from WH Smith's.

"I bought my first Ramones LP from that shop - the first Ramones LP. I was quite late to turn on to the Ramones so this was around late '79 maybe even early 1980.

"The guys who worked in the shop were a few years older than us and were what we would respectfully term proper punks... They were a lot cooler than the hairy bunch down at the bottom of The Moor."

Tony Beesley

"The other Sheffield record shops I remember were one at the back of The Moor that we nick-named the ted shop, as it always seemed full of teddy boys who would eye us up with distrust."

Tony Beesley

Below: Looking down The Moor, 24th November, 1971

Tony Beesley: Punk and shopping at Virgin

"Over the other side at Smith's, one October 'potato peeling week' off school, me and two of my mates found a brand new crispy £20 note pleading for us to pick it up and spend on records.

"No-one was trying to compete with us for our booty so off we went with our plunder and eventually, following some conscience-pricking attempts by one of the lads' parents, we went ahead and bought our spoils; I got the first UK Subs LP released that very week on blue vinyl and a selection of Revolution shop cheapies. Teenage years just couldn't get much better than this could they?

"The other Sheffield record shops I remember were one at the back of The Moor that we nick-named the ted shop, as it always seemed full of teddy boys who would eye us up with distrust but luckily never to my knowledge seriously gave us much grief, apart from the usual Punk hate comments. We didn't buy that much from there. The record sleeves were always really tatty and that Starjets single that had only been out a few weeks looked as vintage as the rock'n'bopping clientele.

"The other old chestnut was Rare and Racy right at the top of Division Street. For a few years that shop provided us with scores of albums at the set price of £2.30. That price never increased through the Thatcher years of increased inflation and beyond and for me personally, and I am sure for some of my punk-loving pals, threw me the final few pieces of the punk vinyl collection jigsaw.

"LPs that we had either not been able to afford, weren't sure of their musical worth or had completely missed out on through stupidity or ignorance were there for the taking.

"Penetration's Moving Targets LP on clear and crackly vinyl for £2.30 anyone?"

Meat and potato pie at Wapentake Bar

Chapter 9

Olga Marshall in residence at Wapentake Bar

Olga Marshall: Wapentake Bar dinners

> "Coming to Wapentake Bar was considered a 'bit of dare' for some people as we'd got a jukebox."
>
> **Olga Marshall**

Olga Marshall, former manager of seventies dinner time haunt Wapentake Bar, said:

"We were renowned for serving up homely food – we were very popular with pensioners and shop and office workers. Meat and potato pie was one of our best sellers together with long sausages in bread-sticks. We also did cottage pie and salads.

"Coming to Wapentake Bar was considered a 'bit of dare' for some people as we'd got a jukebox [the venue was a rock bar by night] but I managed to build a strong customer base.

"We became a meeting place for pensioners and served cheap meals.

"We also became a popular destination for the Telegraph's 'women's circle'

for two or three years.

"I teamed up with the Cineplex and, for 99p each, the ladies would get lunch at Wapentake Bar, a tour of the hotel upstairs and then get to see a film. I'd also sometimes give them a sherry from the hotel's cocktail bar.

"A lot of office workers liked the atmosphere we'd got and the fact they could play table football."

Olga Marshall

Above: Wapentake Bar entrance in the seventies.

Left: Olga Marshall at Wapentake Bar (left) with future Limit club owner George Webster (far right)

A well-stocked stall in Sheffield markets in the early 1970s

Chapel Walk in the seventies

Sexy Rexy and more Moor

Chapter 10

Julie Spafford in the seventies

Mr Harry is not a big shirt-maker. He makes shaped shirts to make you slim. Super-shaped shirts if you are slim. And not many of either. Mr. Harry® creates original designs in a Limited Edition —and that's it. The only thing he's consistent about is quality.

Mr Harry

LIMITED EDITION

®Registered Trade Mark

PAUL REX IS SEXY REXY

Charles Street, Sheffield, and 22, Howard Street, Rotherham.

Julie Spafford: Bleached jeans

"Sexy Rexy, I remember it well.

"You went in this dark, psychedelic shop and bought an expensive pair of men's Levi or Wrangler indigo coloured jeans only to take them home and either lie in the bath with them on to make them fit a woman's hips and bottom or pour bleach on them to make the dark blue lighter! There were no jeans for women and no other colours than the dark blue.

"I remember buying one particular pair and the stitching came undone. I took them back and the manager hid behind a dummy whilst his staff told me they did not do refunds, even on faulty goods, so I went and stood in the doorway advising everyone who came into the shop that they only sold shoddy goods and not to shop there.

"The manager was there like a shot!"

Debbie Ogden

"I was one of the 'ABC Minors' when I was a kid.

"We'd queue up the alley near Cockaynes to get in. My mum used to put us in there whilst she went shopping.

"We'd watch the likes of Laurel and Hardy and Abbott and Costello.

"When you got older you went to the Top Rank.

"I remember seeing Slade, Gary Glitter and Showaddywaddy on a Saturday afternoon there."

GRAND OPENING OF JUST PANTS AT 31/35 THE MOOR, SHEFFIELD AT 1·30 P.M. ON THURSDAY NOV. 29TH

BY SHEFFIELD UNITED FOOTBALL TEAM

WE'RE PACKED WITH THE LATEST GEAR

OVER 2,000 PAIRS OF FASHION PANTS AND JEANS IN FOUR LEG LENGTHS, 26"-40" WAIST.

OVER 1,000 TRENDY SHIRTS, INCLUDING JP PLUS, BEN SHERMAN, REVELATION AND JAYTEX DESIGNS.

10% DISCOUNT OFF ALL PURCHASES IF YOU BRING THIS ADVERTISEMENT WITH YOU. FIRST SEVEN DAYS ONLY.

GUINEA GIFT REDUCTION

on all perm waving during the month of January, on the first four days of each week.

Let our expert stylists create your new hair style with a Cream Perm Wave to keep it looking at its best. Late nights Thursday and Friday.

George France
HAIR ARTIST
23, CHAPEL WALK, SHEFFIELD, 1.
PHONE 77616/7/8.

Joanne Stephenson:

"I remember getting my first pair of drainpipe jeans and sitting in the bath in them when I got home so they'd mould to me! I needed a coathanger to help do the zip up they were that tight! "

Val Wilkinson: In the Sexy Rexy warehouse

Val Johnson (now Wilkinson)

"I had a job in the Sexy Rexy warehouse in Heeley. I used to put the prices tags on the clothes. We'd regularly work until 2 o'clock in the morning – there was always so much to do.

"The shop was very famous for Levi jeans – it was a very busy place. They were nice the Caplan brothers that owned it. They're tycoons in property now I think. My niece went out with Rex.

"The Sexy Rexy shop was very arty with wooden floors and hundreds of pairs of jeans.

"Sheffield was fantastic in the seventies.

"I remember having friends visiting me from London and they expected it to be nothing but chimney pots. They were shocked that it was big and bustling and the people were so friendly.

"Shops like Walshs and Cockaynes were buzzing and we had great nightclubs like The Fiesta and Baileys."

Val Wilkinson
in the seventies

Val Wilkinson today

"The Sexy Rexy shop was very arty with wooden floors and hundreds of pairs of jeans.

"I remember having friends visiting me from London and they expected it to be nothing but chimney pots."
Val Wilkinson

Chapel
Walk, 1977

No talking at Philip Cann

Chapter 11

Chapel Walk seen here on a wet day in the seventies

Moorfoot traffic - the new Moorfoot road junction

Pollards in Broomhill

"We had to play classical music all the time but on Miss Hinch's day off we went mad and played pop records."

Sheryl Littlewood

Left:
Philip
Cann

Sheryl Littlewood: Shop assistant at Philip Cann

Sheryl Littlewood today

Sheryl Littlewood: "I was a shop assistant at the record department of Philip Cann on Chapel Walk. It was downstairs and there were no windows – it was a very big area.

"The management were very old school and very old. I remember my boss Miss Hinch, she was like a school ma'am.

"We weren't even allowed to talk to our fellow shop assistants!

"We had to play classical music all the time but on Miss Hinch's day off we went mad and played pop records.

"I was 17 when I started and very rebellious. I arrived in a mini-skirt and high heels.

"Football star Tony Currie was a regular.

"The biggest record at the time was Tubular Bells by Mike Oldfield.

"We'd be packed solid on a Saturday afternoon and our biggest rivals were Wilson & Pecks. I earned £12 a week. Before that I was a hairdresser earning just £8 a week.

"I remember one day someone pinched a TV. Everybody thought the guy was an engineer. He just walked in, picked it up, and walked off with it!

"Very little got pinched thankfully.

"We also had a music department that sold instruments and sheet music."

Sheryl in the early seventies

Above: Woolworths on The Moor and, below, inside the store

Wilson Peck

Orchard Street

Cockaynes on Angel Street

Thomas Wallhead: From shop assistant to managing director

Thomas Wallhead, 96, joined Cockaynes as a shop assistant in 1934. He dedicated his life to the family department store and rose through the ranks to become managing director.

He stayed to oversee its takeover by Schofields in 1972.

Cockaynes was founded by two brothers in 1829 on Angel Street.

Farewell gifts given by staff and management at Thomas's retirement party included a Royal Doulton dinner service, a cassette recorder, rocking chair and greenhouse.

Jean Lees, Thomas's daughter, said: "Walshs was the main rival - we never dared shop there; or if we did, we had to hide the bags! My dad had a very 'walk and talk' management style - that's probably why he's so fit now at 96."

Thomas Wallhead in recent years

The Cockayne family will make their last break with Schofields Department Store, formerly T B and W Cockayne Ltd, Sheffield, later this month when the general manager, Mr John Cockayne leaves the firm.

T B and W Cockayne Ltd was founded by two brothers in 1829 on the site of the present store in Angel Street.

Mr Cockayne agreed to stay on following Schofields' take-over to provide continuity and help with the transition.

He will leave the firm on August 17 after working at the store for 11 years.

He said yesterday : "I have not yet decided what I will be doing in the future."

The present assistant general manager, Mr T H Wallhead, will take over as general manager,

Mr T H WALLHEAD

JOHN COCKAYNE

responsible to the board in Leeds.

He joined Cockaynes in 1934 and was appointed director in charge of furnishings in 1954.

Sweet sixteen on the cosmetics counter

Chapter 12

The resplendent
Walshs department
store on 10th Feb 1972

Atkinsons

"Marti Caine was a regular - she always looked so glamorous."

Angela McBroom

Angela McBroom: Working in Schofields

Angela McBroom: "I worked in the cosmetics department at Schofields. I started at 15 and was one of the youngest there. We were like one big family in there.

"There'd be one girl on each 'house': one on Revlon, one on Estee Lauder and so on. The hours were 9am to 5.30pm. I started two days before my 16th birthday.

"If you did a big sale on behalf of another girl you'd get a free gift – that would never happen nowadays, you'd probably get the sack for doing it!

"If you got a lady or a man with an account you'd give them special treatment. Nowadays people don't want accounts.

"In those days we'd have to wear that much make-up we'd look like dolls!

"Marti Caine was a regular – she always looked so glamorous.

"I'd regularly eat my sandwich at dinnertime sat on the wall outside the Dove and Rainbow.

"I'd normally go to The Attic sandwich shop that was opposite Rebina shoes and buy one of their crusty sandwiches – they were the biggest things you've ever seen!"

Knitwear ALL £1·75

Peter Robinson department store.

Walshs

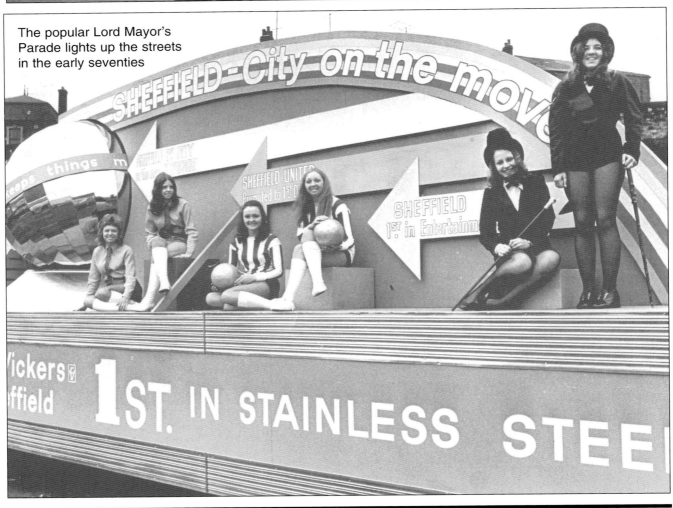

The popular Lord Mayor's Parade lights up the streets in the early seventies

A busy
Fargate
in 1978.

Eyeing up the fireworks on 25th October 1972

The Moor

The Moor

Winning the pools and Wigfalls

Chapter 13

Sadiq Malik in his Glen Road corner shop, Nether Edge. 5th March 1976

Mrs Florence Thackeray – proud owner of Sheffield's smallest shop of the time (Sept 1977) on Upper Hanover Street

H. Savage of 480 London Road in February 1977

Jackson The Tailor of Fargate in January 1978

Janet Marcon: Working in the city centre

"I worked in Sheffield city centre for Sun Life of Canada which was situated above what was I think the gas board showroom on the corner of Church Street and Fargate, or Coles Corner as it was still known at the time.

"I remember Rackhams replacing Walshs – Walshs always being classed as the 'posh' shop more for older people with money. I actually bought some trousers from there once that cost £40, a lot of money in those days.

"Down Snig Hill where Argos is now was Cockaynes, which was owned by a local Sheffield family, I think.

"It was a beautiful shop with fitted carpets and it sold everything a department store should.

"Of course there was no tram in those days – buses had replaced the old versions and Supertram was years away – so you could actually drive through the centre of Sheffield and, believe or not, park!

"Down in Fitzalan Square was the main post office, the old Cartoon Cinema, Wigfalls department store. My father actually worked for Wigfalls for 25 years; they were another local family firm.

"I bought a bedroom suite from that shop in 1971. I won the pools earlier that year and could afford to buy a lot of new things.

"I also bought a pram for my first child and got discount because of dad's position.

"On one occasion my fiancé picked me up from work in his 'sit up and beg' style Ford Anglia. He parked it in Fitzalan Square alongside the old Police Box that used to be there and we went to the cinema. When we came out the car had gone.

"He went to the police station after he put me on a bus home: I remember being scared walking down Millhouses Lane as it was dark and only lit by the old standard lights.

"We'd been to see Alfred Hitchcock's The Birds. It was all very eerie and I remember hearing owls hooting. The car was later found, in Nottingham."

> "I remember Rackhams replacing Walshs – Walshs always being classed as the 'posh' shop more for older people with money."
> **Janet Marcon**

Turners Shoes in Hillsborough

Suggs and Barney Goodman sitting either side of the Cambridge Arcade archway in 1975

Christmas shopping and the rise of Challenge

Chapter 14

The Christmas tree is erected in the Hole In The Road.

Telephones: Sheffield 78585 General: 26393 Personal Announcements and Want-Ads

It's the big city switch-on

THOUSANDS SEE LIGHTS AS SHEFFIELD TURNS INTO SEA OF COLOUR

By a staff reporter

BARKER'S POOL was turned into its traditional sea of colour last night as thousands of people gathered for the switch-on of Sheffield's Christmas Lights by Lord Mayor Ald. Sidney Dyson.

Just to make sure everything went according to plan, the Lord Mayor, pictured with Mrs. Dyson, was accompanied by popular comedians Mike and Bernie Winters, and there was an appearance by Father Christmas.

After a few words from

the Lord Mayor and Ald. Reg Munn, chairman of the Illuminations Committee, the lights were turned on six minutes early and followed by a spectacular firework display by members of Sheffield Fire Brigade.

The mile-and-a-half display of lights costing about £15,000, were switched on from the steps of the City Hall.

Before and after the switch-on thousands of people packing Barker's Pool were led through Christmas carols by a massed choir from the city's Stannington Junior School, together with the Sheffield Youth Band.

The guard of honour for the guests on the rostrum, who included the Master and Mistress Cutler, Mr. and Mrs. T. Burleigh, was provided by the Sheffield based 367 Squadron, ATC.

The lights are erected and maintained every year by the highways and lighting section of Sheffield Corporation's Engineers Department.

Santa Claus at The Moor grotto

Fargate at Christmas prior to pedestrianisation

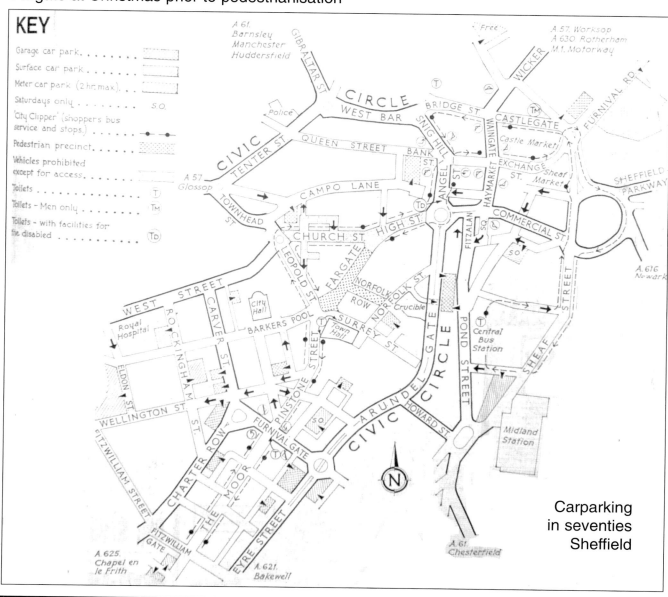

Carparking in seventies Sheffield

CHRISTMAS LIGHTS FUND HITS SAME OLD SNAG

AFTER again giving Sheffield the country's biggest display of Christmas lights members of the Sheffield Illuminations Committee have a problem. The same problem as last year and the year before — cash.

"It can be very disheartening." Mr. W. H. Curtis, chairman of the Lights Appeal sub-committee, said last night.

"We start off well with generous donations of £250 each from such big stores as Coles, Pauldens and Walshs and from Sheffield Newspapers. Industry also plays its part.

"Then the flow of donations begins to fade off and we have to start again the big slog of jogging up those people on the route of the illuminations to send in their donations.

"At the moment we have received £3,000 towards the £5,000 we need to keep faith with the Corporation, which again made a grant of £10,000.

"I appeal to those shops which have not yet made their contribution to do so as soon as possible to relieve our anxieties — not only about this year but whether the lights will go on again next year."

Crowds pack Barkers Pool for the annual light switch on ceremony

Admiring a shop's Christmas display

Cockaynes food court

So Lo Supermarket, Halifax Road in August 1977

Challenge!
SUPERMARKET
849 ECCLESALL ROAD,
GREYSTONES
SHEFFIELD
GRAND OPENING
THURSDAY, DECEMBER 3rd **10** A.M.

THOUSANDS OF DISCOUNT PRICES

| BROOKE BOND PG TIPS TEA 1/3 QTR. (MAX. ½ LB. PER SHOPPER 3 DAYS) | STORK MARGARINE 11 D. ½ LB. | SYMBOL ASSORTED BISCUITS 8/11 3½ LB. TIN | SUGAR 1/- 2 LB. BAG (MAX. 4 LB. PER SHOPPER 3 DAYS) |

MONEY BACK GUARANTEE

| LINCOLNSHIRE KING EDWARD POTATOES 9/11 56 LB. BAG | OPEN UNTIL **8** P.M. EVERY | LATE NIGHT SHOPPING WEDNESDAY THURSDAY FRIDAY | PRIME ENGLISH TOPSIDE OF BEEF 5/- LB. |

FREE CAR PARK — FREE CAR PARK

| JOHN WEST SALMON 4/9 7½ OZS. TIN | ROBERTSONS MINCEMEAT 1/7 14½ OZS. JAR | CIGARETTES 3 D. OFF REC. PRICE ALL 20's | TYPHOO TEA 1/3 QTR. (MAX. ½ LB. PER SHOPPER 3 DAYS) |

ENJOY YOUR SHOPPING IN SUPER SURROUNDINGS

| ROWNTREES JELLIES 10 D. PKT. | MOTORIST SPECIAL! FREE VOUCHER WORTH 1/- GIVEN TO THE FIRST 10,000 CUSTOMERS Redeemable when you buy 3 gallons of petrol at GREYSTONES B.P. FILLING STATION, adjacent to Challenge Supermarket valid until 12th DECEMBER, 1970 | SAILORS SPECIAL! WIN A FABULOUS POLYCELL PIONEER SAILING DINGHY SEE DETAILS OF THIS COMPETITION AT CHALLENGE SUPERMARKET COMPETITION ENDS 12th DECEMBER | VIM CANISTER (L'GE). 11 D. |

SAVE YOUR MONEY **Challenge!** SAVE YOUR MONEY

ADVERTISING FEATURE

Luxury shopping at Sheffield's new supermarket

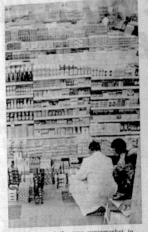

Stocking up at the new supermarket in Ecclesall Road.

Sizing up some of the delicious

YOU CAN'T hitch your horse to a post outside a new supermarket in Ecclesall Road.

But you can do the next best thing — and tie your dog to the specially provided "doggy rail."

It's just one of the useful services which Challenge are providing to ensure that they have satisfied customers in this, their biggest supermarket store yet.

Mr. Geoffrey Elliott Geen, managing director of the company, emphasised that the "doggy rail" is not a gimmick.

"We don't believe in gimmicks, we believe in giving value for money," he said.

"And it is in this context that we are providing OUTSIDE accommodation for dogs."

Mr. Geen said that he was very much against dogs wandering round food stores, but he appreciated that many customers did not like leaving their pets at home.

REPUTATION

It was exactly twelve months ago that the first Challenge supermarket was opened in the Sheffield area, at Manor Top, City Road.

It has a sales area of 7,000 square feet and every week, since the opening, it has attracted many thousands of customers.

There is no doubt that the reputation established at Manor Top will stand the Ecclesall Road venture in good stead.

The new store has a sales floor area of over 15,000 square feet and is equipped with the latest equipment to ensure that customers will be shopping in absolute luxury.

Designed by the Raven Design Group of Sutton-in-Ashfield, it is the second Sheffield supermarket to be completed within a month by F. P. A. Finnegan Ltd whose own elegant 15,000 square feet seven storey headquarters building faces across the Ecclesall Road supermarket's wide parking lot.

Hillards 15,000 square feet building at Sheffield Lane Top was built in only seven months; the Ecclesall Road building which is much bigger at a total of 26,000 square feet has taken nine months.

Mr. Geen claims for it: "We are offering probably a wider range of goods than any similar operation in the North of England.

By a staff reporter

"Foodstuffs, plus thousands of non-food lines, including car accessories, paint, greeting cards, a unique range of top quality house plants and many other special features.

"All these things, and many others, are here for people to purchase."

This particular supermarket firm has always specialised in fresh cut foods such as fresh meat and Mr. Geen sets great importance on the "over-the-counter" service which will be available.

"We shall have a full range of fresh cheese — not pre-packed — and the same with meat."

UNIQUE

The traditional butcher will still be much in evidence at Ecclesall Road and the butchery department will be prepared to cut the smallest portions for people like old age pensioners or those living on their own.

Mr. Geen regards this as an important service when so much pre-packed food has a minimum weight level below which it is not available.

Also there is no increase in price for the smaller portions. Pro rata, it works out exactly the same as buying larger quantities — a boon again for the old age pensioner on a limited income.

The range of cheeses is also going to be a boon to those who, like me, find a great deal of difficulty in finding decent cheese which hasn't been prepacked, pre-wrapped and pre-de-flavoured!

According to Mr. Geen there will be "a fantastic range" of English and Continental cheeses, and customers will be able to choose exactly the piece they want from the gleaming refrigerated display case.

Other items on offer will include freshly-roasted chicken, available daily to take home hot; fresh cream cakes served from a refrigerated case to ensure freshness and hygiene; and hot bread which will be available every day.

And while mother is doing the shopping, father can wander round the non-grocery items. The motorist, for example, will find much to interest him on the shelves.

Then, as you leave the store, you pass through the modern fresh fruit and vegetable section.

'HEAT WALL'

It's the final point before passing through a "heat wall" to the outside.

And another proud boast:

There will be no waiting at check-outs.

As one who has suffered the interminable wait in a queue of shopping trolleys, I can only hope that Mr. Geen's optimism is well-founded.

Certainly the ten gleaming payout points look as though they will be able to deal with the shopping public and Mr. Geen has the flexibility among his

staff to ensure that peak periods can be dealt with.

In fact he is prepared to approve the use of not just one packer, but two, to help speed the flow when things get really hectic.

FUNCTION

One of the most important functions in a supermarket — or any store for that matter — is that of collecting the money.

It's important for the shop itself, but it's equally important for the customer, who has to place a considerable amount of trust in the payout girls.

One slip of the finger on the adding machine keyboard can prove expensive.

In fact there are gadgets on the market today which enable shoppers to add up their grocery bill as they gather the various items.

Then, when they receive their bills, they can check their total against the amount on the cash register.

As decimalisation is introduced, this gadget should prove invaluable.

The need for it at the new store is almost certain to be purely academic. Already the team of payout girls are being specially trained by a representative of the cash register firm.

"We make a point of bringing in an expert seven days before the opening to show the girls how the machines operate and other facets of the job.

"They are also getting a thorough training in decimalisation conversion."

POLICY

And on the subject of conversion, Mr. Geen states that, as a matter of policy, his organisation will only give the new currency in change after Decimalisation Day.

Of course, there will be nothing to stop customers proffering the old coinage, but if all the shops and stores take the same line (and the Sheffield

Chamber of Trade president, Mr. Chris Day, is advocating this at his store), the switchover will perhaps be rather more speedy than Government pronouncements have led us to expect.

The new supermarket will employ a staff of about 80 people, most of whom will be locally recruited.

Not only will it provide an important shopping outlet, and perhaps muchneeded keener price competition in the grocery world, but it will play its small part in helping to make Sheffield one of the best cities in the country so far as shopping and employment is concerned.

Trolley shopping in comfort.

The Manager

THE MANAGER of the new supermarket, Mr. Colin Mayor, learned the grocery industry the hard way in a market hall.

He has trained in every aspect of the industry from being a boy on a market stall in Bolton.

He has been in the grocery retail trade since he left school 13 years ago, and before taking up his present promotion, was an area manager with the company.

A married man with two children, Mr. Mayor lives at North Anston, moving there from Leeds recently.

He is full of enthusiasm for his new job, and describes the Ecclesall Road store as one of the best in the city.

"We want to establish a good relationship with the customers, and we hope to carry on the tradition established at Manor Top, where we have always tried to give a first-class service."

An article from The Star of Wednesday, December 2, 1970

The mighty Challenge Supermarket

Inside Challenge Supermarket Ecclesall Road 30th November 1970

Sheffield markets

Chapter 15

Market at Moorfoot in 1976.

Sheffield Rag and Tag Market

Sheffield markets area on a sunny day in the seventies

Woolco Department Store

Flea Market in July 1977

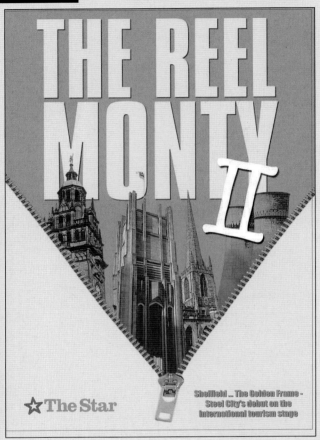
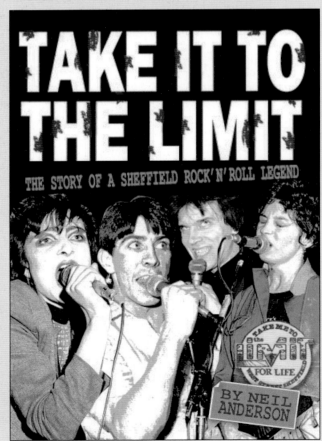
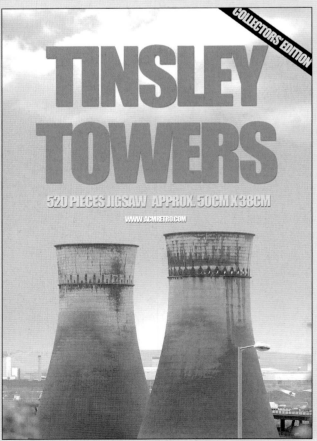